CW00607154

Step by Step
with
Jesus

*Written by Narelle Gatenby and
Eric Bird/Illustrated by Peter Oram*

AN ALBATROSS BOOK

the bible reading fellowship
MAKING SENSE OF THE BIBLE

© Narelle Gatenby and Eric Bird 1988

Published in Australia and New Zealand by
Albatross Books Pty Ltd
PO Box 320, Sutherland
NSW 2232, Australia
in the United States of America by
Albatross Books
PO Box 131, Claremont
CA 91711, USA
and in the United Kingdom by
The Bible Reading Fellowship
Peter's Way, Sandy Lane West
Oxford OX4 5HG, England

First edition published by Monarch Productions 1988
Second edition (completely revised) 1992
Reprinted 1992

*This book is copyright. Apart from any fair
dealing for the purposes of private study,
research, criticism or review as permitted
Under the Copyright Act, no part of this book
may be reproduced by any process without
the written permission of the publisher.*

National Library of Australia
Cataloguing-in-Publication data

Gatenby, Narelle
Step by Step with Jesus

ISBN 0 86760 109 4 (Albatross)
ISBN 0 7459 1712 7 (BRF)

1. Jesus Christ 2. Bible — Study and teaching
I. Bird, Eric. II. Title

232

Scripture quotes in this book are from the *Good News Bible*,
© American Bible Society 1966, 1971, 1976.
Printed and bound in Australia by The Book Printer, Victoria

Contents

INTRODUCTION: *Finding your way*

To help us find our way in the Bible each book is divided into **chapters** and **verses**.

If there is more than one book or letter by the same name, the number 1, 2, or 3 is written before it.

This is the *name of the book*. It tells what the book is about, or who wrote it, or to whom it was written. This is the Good News of Jesus, written by Luke.

The text of each book is set out in *columns* for easy reading. Read down the column and continue at the top of the next column.

The *last chapter* on each page is written here.

Verse numbers are written in small print.

Chapter numbers are written in large print.

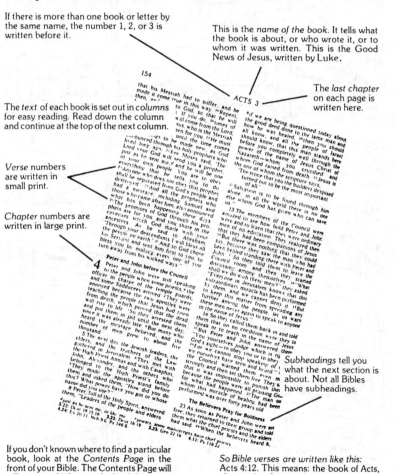

Subheadings tell you what the next section is about. Not all Bibles have subheadings.

If you don't known where to find a particular book, look at the *Contents Page* in the front of your Bible. The Contents Page will tell you on which *page* the book begins.

So Bible verses are written like this: Acts 4:12. This means: the book of Acts, chapter 4 and verse 12.

THE BIBLE IS A LIBRARY

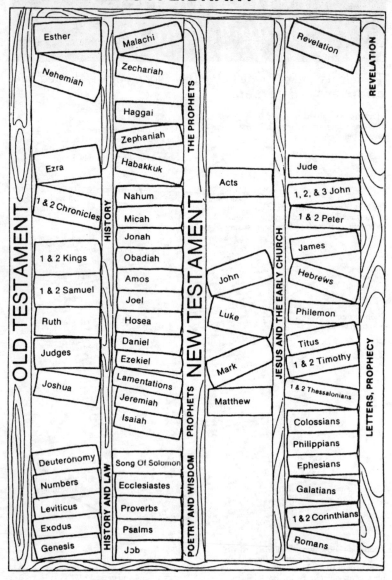

STUDY ONE:
Messengers of good news

Two thousand years ago, there was born a man whose life changed the direction of the world. His birth was a turning point in history. Years are numbered from his birth. More books have been written about him than about any other man. Wars have been fought, laws passed and nations formed in his name. Yet he lived only about thirty-four years, he died a criminal's death and his life was reliably recorded by only four writers. His name is Jesus.

Before we begin looking at the life and claims of Jesus, we should consider the men who gave us our information about him. Who were they? Can we trust them? How well did they know Jesus and why did they write about him? Their reports about Jesus are called 'Gospels' or 'announcements'.

DAY ONE:
Matthew 9: 9–12

1. The first Gospel we find in the Bible was written by Matthew. Many believe that he was the man who became Jesus' disciple. What did he do for a living (verse 9)? _____

2. How do we know from verse 10 that Matthew was glad to have Jesus as his friend?

_____

 DAY TWO:
Matthew 13: 45–46

Matthew was impressed by Jesus' teaching. He took care to collect the word-pictures and main themes Jesus taught the people. These word-pictures are called *parables*. They are stories from everyday life which teach us about God.

3. Look at chapter 13 of Matthew's Gospel and read the headings which are in dark print (use a *Good News Bible*). What are the names of any three of the parables in this chapter?

☐ _____
☐ _____
☐ _____

4. Read the little parable of the pearl in verses 45–46.
    (a) What picture is used to describe the kingdom of heaven (verse 45)? _____

    _____

    (b) The 'kingdom of heaven' is the rule of God in the lives of people. How valuable, or precious, is the kingdom of heaven (verse 46)?

    _____

 DAY THREE:
Mark 1: 14–18

Mark wrote the Gospel placed second in the New Testament. He was a young lad during the three years of Jesus' ministry. He probably knew Jesus (Mark 14: 51–52), but was not one of his twelve followers or disciples. From the earliest times of the church, it was accepted that Mark wrote down the facts given to him by Peter (1 Peter 5: 13). Peter, James and John were the three disciples closest to Jesus.

5. From verse 16 finish these sentences:
    Simon Peter made his living by _____
    His brother's name was _____
    They fished on Lake _____

6. What was Jesus' message to the people (verse 15)?

    _____

 # DAY FOUR:
Luke 1: 1–4

The writer of the third Gospel was Luke, a doctor (Colossians 4: 14). He didn't know Jesus and did not come from Judea, the place where Jesus lived.

7. Why did Luke write his Gospel (verse 4)?

    _____

8. How do we know Luke took great care to be accurate — no gossip, no exaggerating (verse 3a)?

9.   What kind of report did Luke want to write about Jesus (verse 3b)? _____
_____

 DAY FIVE:
John 20: 30–31; John 21: 25

Many people believe that John, the writer of the fourth Gospel, was a disciple and close friend of Jesus. (See Introduction to DAY THREE.)

10.   In chapter 20, verse 30, John tells us he didn't write an account of everything Jesus had said and done. In chapter 21, verse 25 he tells us why he didn't. What was that reason (21: 25)? _____
_____

11.   What does John want us to know about Jesus (verse 31a)? _____

'Messiah' and 'Christ' both mean 'the person God promised he would send'.

12.   What is definitely ours if we put our trust in Jesus (verse 31b)? _____

✎ DAY SIX:

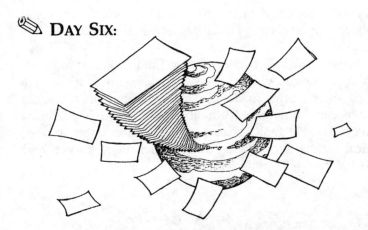

Each writer had an aim of his own. In each of the questions below, write the aim of each Gospel writer.

13. (Matthew 1: 16b) Matthew wants us to know that Jesus is the _____

14. (Mark 1: 1) Mark wants us to know that Jesus is the _____

15. (Luke 1: 4) Luke wrote his Gospel so that _____ _____

16. (John 20: 31) The events John chose to record were written so that _____ _____ _____

✎ SUMMARY

The story of Jesus has been handed down to us with total reliability by men who lived, ate, worked and travelled with Jesus for three years. That's long enough to know if someone is really who he says he is, especially if he says he is the Son of God. Jesus inspired these men to leave everything, risk death and prison for what they were convinced was true. Their claim? God has come among us as this man, Jesus.

Hearing these reports a doctor, Luke, decided to check them out. He interviewed the people who knew Jesus. He studied their stories in detail. He says his reason was so that we can know the truth about what we have heard (Luke 1: 4). He took great care to mention dates, places, political events and people, all of which were known and could be checked by his readers.

These are men who knew the truth about Jesus. It was truth that demanded action from those who heard it. As John says: '. . .these are written that you may believe that Jesus is the Christ, the Son of God, and that by believing you may have life in his name.'

STUDY TWO:
Jesus — no ordinary child

The place is Judea, a little province of little importance in the vast empire of Rome. Judea has been ruled by the occupation armies of Rome and their puppet kings since it was conquered in 63 BC. There has been a number of uprisings. They have all been brutally put down. An unsteady calm exists.

For hundreds of years the Jews have been bullied, ruled and owned by different invaders, but this has only made them more determined to be free. And there is hope. Their holy writings tell them that one day their God will send someone to rescue them. They call him the 'Messiah' which means 'the one who is set apart, or anointed, by God'. He will rescue his people, judge his enemies and rule the nations with the very authority of God himself. He will be like their greatest king, David, but even greater than he was. If only God would act *now*!

But first it is necessary to prepare the right people to take part in his plan. What kind of people would you expect God to choose? They were ordinary people, willing to adjust their way of thinking to fit in with the way God wanted things to be. They were teachable, not stubbornly holding on to their own ideas or insisting on having their own way. They were humble, willing to look foolish if that's what it took for God's plan to succeed.

And so it was that God chose an old childless couple, a young girl and a village carpenter to put into action his plan for the rescue — not only of the Jews, but of the whole human race.

✎ DAY ONE:
God prepares
his people
Luke 1: 5–17

1. What does verse 6 tell us about Zechariah and Elizabeth?

   _____

   _____

   _____

2. What happened while Zechariah was serving in the temple (verse 11)?

   _____

3. What was the angel's message to Zechariah (verse 13)?

   _____

   _____

4. What was John's work to be (verse 17)?
   - ☐ _____
   - ☐ _____
   - ☐ _____
   - ☐ _____

✎ DAY TWO:
God prepares Mary
Luke 1: 26–38

5. What three things did the angel Gabriel tell Mary about her son in verse 32?
   - (a) _____
   - (b) _____
   - (c) _____

6. What did Gabriel tell Mary about her son's kingdom (verse 33)? _____

   _____

7. Describe in your own words how Mary accepted God's plan for her (verse 38). _____

   _____

8. What impresses you most about Mary? _____

   _____

   _____

DAY THREE:
God prepares Joseph
Matthew 1: 18–25

Joseph was betrothed to Mary. Betrothal was more than just an engagement. It was a firm contract and to break it was the same as divorce.

If a man found that the girl to whom he was betrothed had been unfaithful to him, he could take her to court. The punishment could be death. Mary is pregnant and Joseph knows the baby is not his.

9. How did the angel reassure Joseph (verse 20)?

_____

10. What name was Joseph to give the baby (verse 21)?

_____

Why?_____

11. Read verses 19 and 24–25. Why do you think God chose Joseph to look after Mary and his Son?

    _____

    _____

12. *Think:* Can God trust me to care for the people he has given me?_____

    _____

DAY FOUR:
God becomes man
Luke 2: 1–7

13. What political event made Joseph and Mary go to Bethlehem (verses 1–3)?

    _____

    _____

    _____

14. Two prophecies about Jesus' birth are shown to have come true in verse 4. What are they?
    (a) Micah 5: 2

    _____

    _____

    (b) Isaiah 9: 7 and 11: 1, *Good News Bible*

    _____

    _____

15. What importance do you see in the fact that God chose a stable rather than a palace for his Son's birth?

    _____

    _____

DAY FIVE:
Good news for shepherds
Luke 2: 8–20

16. Who is the good news for (verse 10)? _____
_____

17. What is the good news (verse 11)? _____
_____

18. How did the shepherds show that they believed
what the angels had told them (verse 15)?
_____

19. What effect did the shepherd's visit have on:
(a) Mary (verse 19)?
_____

(b) the shepherds themselves (verse 20)?

_____

✎ DAY SIX:
Good news for strangers
Matthew 2: 1–13

20. Where had the strangers come from (verse 1b)?

_____

21. Who did they believe the baby to be (verse 2a)?

_____

22. Why had they come (verse 2b)? _____

_____

23. Compare this with King Herod! Who did he believe the baby to be (verse 4)? _____

_____

24. Why did he want to find him (verse 13)?

_____

25. For the wise men, the birth of Jesus was 'good news'; for King Herod it was 'bad news'. For most of the people of Bethlehem it was 'business as usual'. What does the birth of Jesus mean to you?

_____

_____

_____

✎ SUMMARY

Imagine the spectacle the God of all creation could have put on to announce the arrival of his Son on earth! But that isn't the way God works. We catch only a glimpse of heaven bursting with joy as angels sing and a star first heralds the news to the nations.

A baby boy sleeps in a feedbox, in a village outback in the Roman Empire. He is the Son of God, but only an old couple, a village carpenter and a young girl know the secret. It is a secret shared with a few men minding some scrubby sheep, and some foreigners who dared to risk danger, search and ask questions until they found the truth they were looking for.

The God of history hasn't changed. He still works within the world he has made. He shows himself to those who will listen and he works in the lives of those who will trust and obey. The birth of Jesus, the Messiah — God-be-come-man — happened while dictators raged, politicians ruled and the religious leaders concentrated on keeping their traditions. It was the humble, ordinary people who saw what God was intending to do — how through the baby Jesus he would carry out his rescue operation for all mankind.

STUDY THREE:
Jesus — God become man

We hear little more about Jesus until he is about thirty years old and ready to begin his public ministry. His relative, John, the son of Elizabeth and Zechariah, has gained himself quite a reputation by this time. He is known as 'the Baptiser' because he insists that people be baptised as a sign that they have turned back to God.

He has upset the Jewish leaders. He tells the people that the fact that they are Jews and God's chosen people doesn't make them right with God. He tells them God will only accept them if they have a change of heart. They must turn away from their rebellion against him and ask his forgiveness. He makes quite a stir by announcing 'the Messiah is coming soon, so get ready now!' (Matthew 3: 1–12).

God's rescue mission for the human race is going into action. Crowds come to John to be baptised and among that crowd — quietly, unannounced — comes the One who is himself the only way to God (John 14: 6).

 DAY ONE:
The man with a purpose
Matthew 3: 1–6 and 11–17

1.   Why were people baptised by John (verse 11a)?

_____

2.   John knew that his baptism was just a shadow of what was to come later. What two things did he say about the One who would come after him?
      (a) His baptism (verse 11a)?

_____

(b) His importance (verse 11b)?

_____

3. What did
    Jesus say
    was his
    reason for
    being
    baptised
    (verse 15)?

    _____
    _____
    _____
    _____

4. Here is a
    wonderful
    picture of
    God in three
    persons, or
    the Trinity, each giving witness to God's plan for
    the rescue of mankind (verses 16–17). Finish these
    sentences, showing the part each Person took in the
    baptism of Jesus.
    (a) John saw Jesus, God the Son (verse 16a)

_____

    (b) John saw God the Holy Spirit (verse 16b)

_____

    (c) John heard God the Father say (verse 17)

_____

 DAY TWO:
The man under pressure
Matthew 4: 1-11; Hebrews 4: 15

Jesus is preparing to begin his mission. His baptism is still fresh in his mind — God the Father has confirmed that Jesus is in fact his Son. Satan then tempts Jesus, 'If you are who you say you are, then prove it!'

5.   When did Satan come to Jesus (verses 2–3a)?

_____

6.   How did Satan tempt Jesus to prove he was God's Son?
     (a) verse 3 _____

     _____

     (b) verses 5–6 _____

     _____

7.   How did Satan tempt Jesus to win the kingdoms of the world (verses 8–9)?

_____

8.   Why is it comforting to know that Jesus was tempted just like we are (Hebrews 4: 15)?

_____

9. On every occasion, how did Jesus overcome Satan (verses 4, 7 and 10)?

_____

10. What are you doing in order to know God's word, so as to use it effectively against Satan?

_____

 ## DAY THREE:
The man for those who seek
John 1: 29 and 35–42

11. Who did John the Baptiser say Jesus was (verse 29a)?

_____

12. He knew why Jesus had come. What was the reason (verse 29b)?

_____

13. At first, John's two followers were curious. What did they call Jesus (verse 38)?

_____

14. How had this understanding grown after they had spent an afternoon with Jesus (verses 40–41)?

_____

15. Who do you say Jesus is?

_____

 ## DAY FOUR:
The man for those who doubt
John 1: 43-51

16. Who did Philip understand Jesus to be (verse 45)?

_____

_____

17. What was Philip's answer to Nathanael's question (verse 46)?

    _____

18. In verse 49 we see that Nathanael had changed his mind about Jesus. What had made him think differently (verses 47–48)?

    _____

19. What does it mean to you that Jesus both knows you and sees you?

    _____
    _____

 ## DAY FIVE:
The man for those who have failed
Matthew 9: 9–13

Tax collectors were hated by the Jews because they worked for the Romans and cheated their own people.

Outcasts were any who, for a number of reasons, were not allowed to take part in Jewish worship.

Pharisees were very careful to keep their religious rules which covered all aspects of everyday life.

20. Who was having dinner with Jesus and his disciples (verse 10)?

_____

21. Why would the Pharisees have been surprised to see Jesus eating with outcasts (verse 11)?

_____

22. For whose benefit did Jesus say he had come (verse 13)?

_____

23. Jesus' words in verse 13 mean: 'I haven't come to call those who already think they are good enough but those who know they have failed to meet God's standards.' This can be either an encouragement to us or a warning. Which is it for you?

_____
Why?

_____

_____

 DAY SIX:
The man who gives direction
Mark 1: 14–20

24. What was the theme of Jesus' preaching (verse 15)?

_____

25. Andrew and Peter owned a fishing business. What would it have cost them to obey Jesus' call (verses 17–18)?

_____

26. What was the job Jesus was calling them to (verse 17)?

_____

27. This passage shows us three steps in our
relationship with Jesus.
(a) Turn away from your sins (verse 15).
(b) Believe the good news (verse 15).
(c) Come with me and I will teach you to catch
people (verse 17). At which step are you?

 ## SUMMARY

How does the Son of God begin his rescue mission? First,
he comes to be baptised. He sets himself apart for the job
ahead of him. By dying on a Roman cross as a criminal,
he will take the punishment we deserve. He, instead of us,
will be cut off from his Father.

He knows what he is doing. He knows what it will
cost him. As he goes away into the wilderness by himself,
Satan lays the full force of his pressure on Jesus. It was real
temptation. It hurt. Jesus felt the pressure just like we do.

He fought it — and he won. His weapon? The same one we have to use, the word of God.

A rescue mission needs a team of well-trained people. Jesus' plan for them was simple: they were to turn the world upside down! What a mixed bunch they were! There were the ones who had been prepared for Jesus' coming by John. There was Nathanael, sour and suspicious. There was Matthew, who had more money than sense and who had been kicked out of the local synagogue. There was Andrew and Peter, who understood that there was more to life than running a successful business. There was only one quality to life they all had: they were teachable, willing to change and grow. That's why they were called 'disciples'. It's a word that means 'pupils' or 'followers'.

Jesus is still the man for anyone who is willing to join his school and start again.

STUDY FOUR:
Jesus – the man who was God

We have seen in the last two studies that Jesus was a real man. He was born and grew up. He was tempted. He felt emotional stress. He felt tired. He spent time with people and ate with them. He was truly a man, not just God pretending to be a man.

However, his followers claimed that Jesus the man was also wholly and truly God: not that he was like God, 'a god' or God's messenger. They were Jews, so there was no doubt in their minds about the fact that there is only one God, whom they knew as Jehovah.

Nevertheless, without changing their minds about that, as they listened to Jesus, learned from him and saw what he did, they came to understand that he is God.

✎ DAY ONE:
Lord of creation
Mark 4: 35–41

1. What was Jesus doing while the storm was raging (verse 38a)?

    _____

2. Remember, these men were experienced sailors. What tells you this was a particularly bad storm (verse 38b)?

   _____

3. How did Jesus respond to their panic (verse 39)?

   _____

4. Why were the disciples afraid (verse 41)?

   _____

✎ DAY TWO:
Lord over matter
Mark 6: 30–44

5. Jesus needed to be alone for a while (verse 31). How did Jesus respond when he saw that the people had followed him (verse 34)?

   _____

6. Why were the disciples worried (verses 35–36)?

   _____

7. How much food did they have among all those people (verse 38)?

   _____

8. What did Jesus do with the little that the disciples were able to give him (verse 41)?

   _____

   _____

9.   What was the result (verses 42–43)?

10. What does it mean to you that Jesus never asks us
     to do something for him without also giving us all
     we need to do it? See verses 37 and 41.

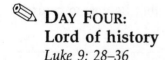

DAY THREE:
Lord over evil
Luke 8: 26–39

11. When the demons recognised Jesus, what were they
     afraid of (verses 28 and 31)?

12. How was the man changed (verse 35)?

13. What command did Jesus give to the healed man
     (verse 39a)?

14. Note verse 39b. What would you tell others that
     'God has done for you'?

DAY FOUR:
Lord of history
Luke 9: 28–36

The Jews' knowledge of God came mainly from 'the law'
and 'the prophets'. God gave the law through Moses.
Elijah was one of the great prophets of God.

15. Who appeared with Jesus and talked with him (verse 30)?

_____

_____

16. What were they talking about (verse 31)?

_____

_____

17. Peter didn't want this wonderful sight to end (verse 33), but God reminds the disciples that his purposes are different from ours. What does God:
    (a) Tell them about Jesus (verse 35a)?

    _____

    (b) Command them to do (verse 35b)?

    _____

 DAY FIVE:
Lord over death
Luke 8: 40–42 and 49–56

18. Why did Jairus come to Jesus (verse 42)?

    _____

19. How did Jesus reassure Jairus that he was in control (verse 50)?

    _____

20. How did the mourners respond when Jesus told them the child's death was only temporary (verses 52–53)?

    _____

21. Describe the child's recovery when Jesus com-

manded life to return to her (verse 55).

_____

_____

_____

 DAY SIX:
Lord of life
John 1: 1–5 and 10–14

22. Who is 'the Word' (verse 14)?

_____

23. Look at these verses and note what they tell us
about 'the Word'.
Verse 1:
(a) _____
(b) _____
(c) _____
Verse 3:
(d) _____
Verse 4:
(e) _____
(f) _____

24. To whom did 'the Word' (Jesus) give the right to be-
     come God's children (verse 12)?

_____

25. It's not enough just to believe about Jesus. We must
     accept him as Lord (boss) of our life if we want to
     be counted as God's children. Have you made that
     commitment of your life to Jesus?

_____

 ## SUMMARY

Jesus showed by what he did that he had all the power of
God at his disposal. He lived and spoke the power of God
with authority and love.

He showed he was *Lord of history* as he spoke with
Moses the lawgiver and Elijah the great prophet. Jesus is
the one to whom the law pointed and about whom the
prophets spoke.

He showed his *power over creation* in stopping the
storm and calming the swelling sea instantly. It is his
creation. It obeys his command. When Jesus took and broke
five bread rolls and two little pickled fish, they became
enough food for 5,000 men (plus women and children).

The forces of evil saw in Jesus their final judgement.
They dared not disobey him. They fled from him,
anywhere as long as it got them out of his presence.

But it is death which is the great and final enemy of
mankind. Here, in the room with Jairus, his wife and their
little girl, Jesus shows that even death is in his power and
must give way to him.

John put it clearly. Jesus is the Word. He is all God
has ever wanted to say to us. The Word, Jesus, is God. Life
is only found in him, and that life brings understanding and
direction to all who put their trust in him (John 1: 1–5).

STUDY FIVE:
Jesus – the way to God

The crowds were thrilled by the miracles Jesus performed. From time to time, they tried to force him to become their king (John 6: 15).

Imagine: a king who could work things so that there was always enough to eat; who could banish sickness from the land; who could 'zap' his enemies and make the nation of Israel great once more! Like a lot of us, they were 'in it for what they could get out of it'. That kind of following doesn't last the distance. Jesus knew it wouldn't.

But there were others: people who saw something more in Jesus than the chance to keep their bellies full and their bank accounts healthy. It wasn't just what Jesus *did* that impressed those people. It was Jesus himself. He was dynamite!

Whenever Jesus had a heart to heart talk with people, he created in them a crisis of conscience. There was something about him they just couldn't ignore. They soon learned that if you had a serious question to ask, you didn't go to Jesus unless you wanted a straight answer.

 DAY ONE:
Jesus and Nicodemus
John 3: 1–21

1. Who was Nicodemus (verses 1 and 10)?

    _____

2. What had impressed him about Jesus (verse 2)?

    _____

3. Finish the sentence:

   Jesus told Nicodemus that no one could see the kingdom of God unless (verse 3):

   _____

4. Jesus used a special name for himself. Nicodemus would have known, by Jesus calling himself by that name, that he was claiming to be the promised Messiah. What was the name he used (verses 13 and 14)? _____

5. Jesus makes some promises for those who are 'born again', those who make him Lord of their life. Note what they are:
   (a) verse 16 _____

   _____

   (b) verse 18 _____

   _____

✑ DAY TWO:
Jesus and the Samaritan Woman
John 4: 5–26 and 28–30; John 7: 38–39

6. What did Jesus say he was able to give to the woman (verse 10)?

_____

_____

7. What results would it have in the life of the one who accepted it (verse 14)?

(a) _____

_____

(b) _____

_____

8. Who is the living water (John 7: 38–39)?

_____

9. What did the woman think Jesus meant (verse 15)?

_____

10. What was the problem in this woman's life (verses 16–18)?

_____

11. The woman began to change the subject away from herself, arguing about where God should be worshipped. What did Jesus say about true worship (verse 24)?

_____

12. Who did Jesus claim to be (verses 25–26)?

_____

DAY THREE:
Jesus and the rich young man
Mark 12: 28–30; Mark 10: 17–22

13.   Which commandment does Jesus
      say is most important (Mark 12:
      29–30)?

      _____

      _____

14.   What did the young man want
      to know (Mark 10: 17)?

      _____

      _____

15.   What did the young man love
      more than he loved God
      (Mark 10: 21–22)?

      _____

In asking the young man to sell his possessions, Jesus was
showing him that he was mistaken in thinking he had kept
all the commandments (verse 20). He had failed to keep
the first and most important one. He didn't love the Lord
with all his heart.

16.   List below the things in your life that are most
      important to you (e.g. career, sport, possessions,
      family).

      _____

      _____

17.   Are any of these things taking you away from your
      commitment to God?

      _____

✎ DAY FOUR:
Jesus and Zaccheus
Luke 19: 1–10

18. Note what each of these verses tells us about Zaccheus:

   verse 2: _____

   verse 3: _____

   verse 7: _____

19. How did Zaccheus feel when Jesus told him he was coming to his house (verse 6)?

   _____

20. What shows that Zaccheus was changed by his meeting with Jesus (verse 8)?

   _____

21. For what reason did Jesus come to his world (verse 10)?

   _____

22. How has meeting Jesus changed you (e.g. your ideas, what you now think is important, how you treat other people, what you want in life)?

   _____

   _____

✎ DAY FIVE:
Jesus and the Pharisees
Luke 19: 48 to 20: 8

The Pharisees were religious Jews who made it their aim to keep every detail of the Jewish law, as well as the traditions and complicated rules that they had built up around it.

23. What was Jesus doing while in the Temple (verse 1)?

   _____

24. What did the people think of Jesus' teaching (Luke 19: 48)?

_____

25. Check Luke 20: 5–7. Which statement best describes the Pharisees (tick the one you choose):
    ❏ They were mostly interested in knowing the truth about God.
    ❏ They were mostly interested in what the people thought about them.
    ❏ They really did listen to Jesus but didn't believe him.

26. Jesus' answer to the Pharisees is the same for everyone who decides not to listen to him. What is it (verse 8)?

_____

27. Jesus' teaching is available for everyone. Is it important how we listen? Why?

_____

_____

✎ Day Six.
Jesus and the woman caught in adultery
John 8: 1–11

28. Why had the Pharisees brought this woman to Jesus (verse 6)?

_____

29. What was the penalty for adultery (verse 5)?

_____

Jesus does not deny the fact that this woman has committed a serious crime. He does condemn the self-righteous attitude of those who have brought her before all these people.

30. How does Jesus show that he upholds the law, but at the same time condemns her accusers (verse 7)?

_____

31. Jesus has given this woman a second chance. What does he tell her to do with it (verse 11)?

_____

32. Jesus gives each one of us the opportunity to 'repent' (turn away from our rebellion against God, accept his forgiveness and begin a new life with Jesus in control).
   What have you done with the opportunity he has given you?

_____

SUMMARY

The amazing thing about Jesus was that no one could fool him. If he was asked a question, he saw past it to the real question. If he wasn't asked a question, he answered the one that should have been asked. He seemed to see right inside people's heads. He knew what made them tick.

For an old man named Nicodemus who had given religion his best shot all his life, Jesus had the alarming news that he had missed the mark completely. He had to be born again.

For a Samaritan woman who had tried to find security in one relationship after another, Jesus had the puzzling news that her security could only come from a change within her, not from other people. She needed God's lifechanging Spirit.

For the rich young man, aware that something in his life was missing, there was the sad news that the eternal life he thought he wanted, he didn't want enough to actually take hold of it. He had to give God first place in his life.

For Zaccheus, whose self-esteem was even smaller than he was, there was the good news that he was loved, accepted and could have a fresh start. His change of heart showed in an immediate change of lifestyle.

For those who wanted an answer, the answer was always the same. To all, in their different needs and with their different questions, the answer was Jesus himself. He is the one who gives new birth, living water, eternal life, forgiveness and full acceptance.

Likewise, for those who would not come, would not see, Jesus always had the same answer: 'For you, there are no answers' (Luke 20: 8). Jesus is the way to God for all who are really wanting to know him.

STUDY SIX:
Jesus and the kingdom of God

It's a sad fact that most people in our own country have never grown up in their knowledge of God. Most know more about cars or sport or TV personalities than they do about the one who made them and who keeps the whole universe ticking along.

Ask the average person the question 'Who was Jesus?' and they may say 'a good man' or 'a good teacher'. Ask them 'What did Jesus teach about?' and the answer will probably be 'Wouldn't have a clue' or 'Do to others what you'd have them do to you'.

The fact is that during the three years Jesus taught, his main theme was the kingdom of God: who could belong to it and what it means to be a citizen of that kingdom. It is a citizenship only open to those who accept it on God's terms. The kingdom of God is his rule in our lives.

It is a theme which is hard. It leaves a lot of people outside and yet the doors are open to all who will enter. Let's look at what Jesus taught about the kingdom of God.

 DAY ONE:
The kingdom of God for those who listen
Matthew 13: 10–17

1. A parable is a story from everyday life which teaches us about heaven. Why did Jesus use stories to teach the crowds (verse 13)?

    _____

2. Why were the crowds so slow to understand about God (verse 15a)?

3. What does Jesus say to those who have listened and begun to understand the word of God (verse 12a)?

4. What does he say to those who will not listen (verse 12b)?

 DAY TWO:
The kingdom of God for those who repent
Luke 15: 11–24

In this story, the son is a picture of any one of us. The father is a picture of God.

5. What did the son do with his money (verse 13)?

6. Where did he finish up (verses 15–16)?

   _____

7. Why did he decide to go home (verse 17)?

   _____

8. How did his father receive him (verses 20 and 22–24)?

   _____

9. Where are you in relationship with God the Father:
   ❏ far away from God?
   ❏ wanting to come home?
   ❏ knowing you have your Father's love and forgiveness?

✎ DAY THREE:
The kingdom of God for those who accept
Matthew 22: 1–10

In this story, the 'king' is a picture of God inviting us to come into his kingdom. The 'son' is Jesus. The 'invited guests' are the Jews and the 'people on the streets' are the rest of the world.

10. Who was giving the feast (verse 2)?

   _____

11. For whom was he giving the feast (verse 2)?

   _____

12. Remember, an invitation from a king is a royal command. How did the invited guests answer the king's invitation (verses 5–6)?

    _____

13. How does verse 7 show us that God ultimately will not put up with rebellion against his authority?

    _____

14. Which kinds of people are invited by God to accept him as king and come to his feast (verse 10)?

    _____

✎ DAY FOUR:
The kingdom of God for those who take root
Matthew 13: 1–9 and 18–23

15. The seed in this story is the word of God. The sower is a picture of those who tell others about God. The different soils are the different people who hear the word of God. Complete the chart below.

    **Name the types of ground
    on which the seed fell:**
    1. verse 4 _____
    2. verse 5 _____
    3. verse 7 _____
    4. verse 8 _____

    What happened to the seed?
    1. verse 4 _____
    2. verse 6 _____
    3. verse 7 _____
    4. verse 8 _____

Which people are like the soils?
1. verse 19 _____
2. verses 20–21 _____
3. verse 22 _____
4. verse 23 _____

16. Right now, which soil are you?

_____

✎ DAY FIVE:
The kingdom of God for those who live it
Luke 10: 25–37

17. Look at verses 25 and 29. The teacher of the Jewish law asked two important questions. What were they?
    (a) _____
    (b) _____

18. Jesus knew the teacher was only pretending, so he told him a story about being real or honest in his relationship with God. Read verses 30–35.
    (a) Who were the religious pretenders in the story (verses 31–32)? (Levites looked after the practical details of temple worship.) _____

    _____

    (b) Who was the 'hero' (verse 33)? (Jews thought God hated Samaritans.) _____

    _____

19. What was Jesus' command to the teacher of the law (verses 36–37)? _____

_____

DAY SIX:
The kingdom of God for those who are ready
Matthew 25: 1–13

In this parable, Jesus is teaching about what it will be like when he comes back to judge the world. He is the 'bridegroom' in the story. We are the 'bridesmaids'.

20.   Why did Jesus call five of the girls 'foolish' (verse 3)?

_____

21.   What did the other five do that was 'wise' (verse 4)?

_____

22.   We cannot depend on others to get us into heaven. How do verses 8–9 show that each person has to make his own preparation to be ready for the rest of forever? _____

_____

23.   What picture is used here to show us that, once Jesus has returned, there are no second chances (verses 10b–12)? _____

_____

24. What is Jesus' warning to us all concerning his return (verse 13)? _____

_____

✎ SUMMARY

A newspaper article told of a young man who tried to enter Britain from Australia. It spoke of how his dreams had been shattered and his money wasted when he was turned away at London immigration and sent back home.

His complaint was that, although he knew he didn't meet British entry requirements, he had told the truth about what he planned to do and he sincerely intended to fix up the requirements once he was in the country. He was given 'the royal order of the boot' — kicked out, sent packing — and there was not a thing he could do about it.

God isn't concerned about why we become citizens of his kingdom. The only condition is that we do so on *his* terms. They are the same terms for everyone. It is the kingdom of God for all who will accept his invitation through Jesus, ask his forgiveness, let his word take root in their lives and live as his kingdom people with Jesus in charge.

It will be no use turning up with bags packed, Colgate smile and all the sincere intentions in the world if we haven't already met God's terms. Jesus decides who will come in and entry is for citizens only.

Are you sure you belong to the kingdom of God?

STUDY SEVEN:
Jesus — the truth about God

Just as there are certain regulations as to who can enter a country, so there are standards of behaviour for those who live there. In certain Arab countries alcohol is forbidden and even a foreigner who breaks the law will suffer the penalty of the law. In Malaysia, a number of Australian and British young men have found to their dismay that they have been sentenced to death for drug smuggling. The fact that they are Australians or British doesn't excuse them or set them apart from Malaysian law.

Jesus taught us what is necessary for us to become citizens in God's kingdom. He also taught us about the culture of God's kingdom. He taught what the lifestyle is like, how God's people behave, about what is important and unimportant, acceptable and unacceptable in the kingdom of God.

Matthew collected all these teachings and put them together. We know them as 'the Sermon on the Mount'.

 ## DAY ONE:
True happiness
Matthew 5: 1–12

1. To whom did Jesus give his Sermon on the Mount (verses 1b–2)?

   _____

   Jesus begins to teach his disciples that God's values are different from ours. We think to gain happiness by grasping at it. Jesus teaches that only God can give true happiness.

2. (a) List some of the things our society tells us will make us happy.

   _____
   _____
   _____
   _____

   (b) Next to each verse in the chart below, note the kinds of people Jesus said are truly happy (blessed, well-off). The first is done for you.
   Note: The 'spiritually poor' are those who know they need God (verse 3).
   To 'mourn' means to care about those who are 'dead' because they are rejecting or ignoring God (verse 4).
   To be a 'peacemaker' (verse 10) means not just to oppose conflict between people, but to work for peace between God and mankind. Peace is not just the absence of war. True peace begins in the hearts of people when they allow God to rule them.

True happiness is.	Those who gain this are:
knowing the kingdom of God belongs to me (verse 3)	the spiritually poor
having God comfort me (verse 4)	
receiving what God has promised (verse 5)	
being fully satisfied by God (verse 6)	
experiencing God's mercy (verse 7)	
seeing God (verse 8)	
having God call me his child (verse 9)	
knowing the kingdom of heaven belongs to me (verse 10)	

(c) Look back over these verses. Who is looking after and rewarding these 'happy' people?

_____

 DAY TWO:
True wealth
Matthew 6: 19–21 and 24–34

3. Why is it foolish to store up possessions, riches and personal importance here on earth (verse 19)?

_____

_____

_____

4. Jesus teaches that what we think about and what we work at is what is really important to us.
Here's a test: What do you think is the most important thing to strive for in life?

_____

In the past week, what have you actually thought most about or given your time to?

_____

Are the two answers the same?

_____

5. What does Jesus say should be our 'number one' concern (verse 33a)?

_____

6. What 'things' (verse 33b) does Jesus promise in return (verse 31)?

_____

 DAY THREE:
True discipleship
Matthew 5: 13–16; John 8: 12

7. What does Jesus say his followers are like?
(a) _____
verse 13
(b) _____
verse 14

8. (a) What do we use salt for?

_____

(b) What do you think it means to be 'salt' as a Christian?

_____

9. Letting our light shine
doesn't mean showing off,
'Bible bashing' or doing
good deeds in order to be
noticed. Ours is a reflected
light. What light should our
lives reflect (John 8: 12)?

   _____

   _____

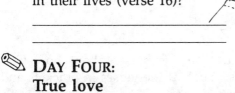

10. Who should be able to see
our light (verse 14a)?

    _____

    _____

11. What is our light meant to do
in their lives (verse 16)?

    _____

    _____

✎ DAY FOUR:
True love
Matthew 5: 38–48; 6: 1–4; 7: 1–5

Those who would follow Jesus must love as he loves.
These passages show us that God's love is different from
ours. Finish the sentences below in your own words:

12. (5: 38–39) People say, 'If someone hurts you, don't
let him get away with it', but God says:

    _____

    _____

13. (5: 40–42) People say, 'Don't let anyone rip you off',
but God says:

_____
_____

14. (5: 43–48) People say, 'Stick by those who'll stick by you', but God says:

_____

_____

15. (6: 1–4) People say, 'Let them see what a good person you are', but God says:

_____

_____

16. (7: 1–5) People say, 'If you don't like him, tell him where to get off', but God says:

_____

_____

 ## DAY FIVE:
True worship
Matthew 6: 5–14; 7: 7–11

These passages give us some promises about how God deals with our prayers. Look at the verses in brackets and then finish the sentences.

17. (6: 5–6) Real prayer doesn't show off, but if we pray with a right attitude to God, he will

_____

18. (6: 14–15) If we forgive others, God will

_____

19. (7: 7–11) We can be sure that, if we ask God for anything that is helpful or that will build us up in our relationship with him, he will

_____

_____

Look at the pattern of prayer Jesus taught his disciples in chapter 6, verses 9–13. (*Note:* only those who can truly call God their Father have the right to pray this prayer.) From the passage, answer the next two questions:

20. If we are Jesus' disciples or followers, what three things will we want for God our heavenly Father?
    (a) verse 9b _____
    (b) verse 10a _____
    (c) verse 10b _____

21. What did Jesus teach us to ask from God?
    (a) verse 11 _____
    (b) verse 12 _____
    (c) verse 13 _____

✎ DAY SIX:
True belonging
Matthew 7: 13–14 and 21–23

22. How does Jesus describe the road to hell (verse 13)?

    _____

23. How does he describe the road to life (verse 14)?

    _____

24. What does Jesus command us to do (verse 13a)?

    _____

25. Look at verses 21–23. Put a tick next to the statement which best describes those who belong to Jesus.
    ❑ They are religious and talk about God (verse 21a).
    ❑ They claim to be God's messengers (verse 22a).
    ❑ They claim to have special spiritual power (verse 22b).
    ❑ Their lives prove that God is their king, because they obey him (verse 21b).

✎ SUMMARY

These words of Jesus are not for
everyone. They are kingdom words for
kingdom people. They were not given
to the crowds, although they were
there and may have heard them.
These were words for Jesus' disciples:
those who were committed to following him and learning from him
(Matthew 5: 1–12).

Becoming a citizen in God's
kingdom means turning away from
our rebellion against God and turning
to a new lifestyle, with new values,
new standards. It is a commitment to letting God remake
us from the inside out. Of course, this takes time.

When new immigrants arrive in our own country, they
are at first very noticeable. They tend to do everything
differently. They don't understand the language, or speak
it with an accent. They don't know the right things to do,
the right places to find help, how to use the banks and
transport.

At first it's quite a struggle, even if their own country
wasn't all that different. They may feel shy, silly, even a
little fearful. If they never settle, they may even decide to
go back to where they came from. In fact, some people
never settle down until they have been back, seen their
former home in a new light and then return happily.

It can be like that for us when we first become citizens
in God's kingdom. Being a Christian is new, unknown,
even a bit frightening. The language seems odd, the people
seem different and we don't know where to go for help.

It's important to keep in mind God's promises and to

see our 'old home' in its true light. Back in the 'old country', people are living for themselves, even though it may be in a 'nice' way; there folk are being driven by their ever-increasing demand for money and possessions; there, it is important who your friends or mates are and whether you're a 'good bloke'. Status is measured by the brand of beer you drink, the car or motorbike you drive, and whether or not you have everything from a video to a holiday house.

In God's kingdom, you're special no matter who you are or where you've come from. You are building up your treasure in heaven. You belong to God; you know his forgiveness, comfort and strength. The kingdom of heaven is yours. God promises to meet all your needs, take you through the hard times, hear your prayers (and always answer) and, finally, to take you home to him.

STUDY EIGHT:
Jesus – the life in God

Jesus had the knack of upsetting some people. The people he upset most were the religious ones — the ones who thought they 'knew it all' about God.

Of course, he upset ordinary people, too, especially when he wouldn't be the kind of Messiah they wanted him to be. He wouldn't be like Santa Claus: put everything right for them and then let them get on with their own lives in their own sweet way.

It wasn't what he *did* that was the problem. He healed the sick, fed the hungry, chased out demons and made the blind see. No, it wasn't what he did. It was what he *said* that was the problem. More to the point, it was what he said about *himself* that worried, angered and upset the opposition.

Jesus made claims about himself that no one in his right mind had ever dared to claim. It was perfectly clear to his Jewish hearers that Jesus was claiming to be equal with God — that is, to be God.

 DAY ONE:
Jesus the Lamb of God
John 1: 29–34

A perfect lamb was often used as an animal for sacrifice. It was killed to 'pay' for the sin of the person who offered it. All these animal sacrifices pointed to the time when God would solve the sin problem once and for all.

1. Why did John call Jesus 'the Lamb of God', the Lamb given by God (verse 29b)?

2. How does John show that Jesus was not just an ordinary man (verse 30)?

3. When a person turned away from his sin and decided to live his life God's way, John would baptise him in the water of the Jordan River. How does Jesus baptise those who come to him (verse 33b)?

4. Why is Jesus able to do this (verse 34)?

If you have accepted God's forgiveness and handed over control of your life to Jesus, then you have been baptised with the Holy Spirit. That means that God the Holy Spirit now lives in you.

✎ DAY TWO:
Jesus – the bread of life
John 6: 28–29 and 35–40

5. What does God want us to do (verse 29)?

6. What does Jesus call himself (verse 35)?

7. What promises does Jesus make to those who put their trust in him?
    (verse 35) _____
    (verse 37b) _____
    (verse 40b) _____

8. Jesus used the ordinary things of life to teach people about their relationship with God. Bread was the basic food of life. Without it people would die of starvation.

   What do you think Jesus meant when he said that those who put their trust in him 'will never be hungry. . . or thirsty' (verse 35)?

   _____

   _____

✎ **DAY THREE:**
Jesus – the good shepherd
John 10: 7–18

9. Jesus uses two pictures to describe himself here. What are they?
   verse 7 _____
   verse 11 _____

10. Why did Jesus come (verse 10b)?

    _____

11. Jesus is telling his disciples that he is going to die, but he wants them to know it is all part of God's plan. How does Jesus reassure them that he is always in control (verse 18)?

    _____

12. If you have put your trust in Jesus, then his death was for you. He is your 'good shepherd'. You are one of his sheep. What does that mean to you personally?

    _____

    _____

    _____

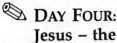

DAY FOUR:
Jesus – the resurrection and the life
John 11: 17–27

Jesus' dear friend, Lazarus, has died (see verses 1–16). Jesus goes to Bethany, near Jerusalem, to bring him back to life (see verses 38–44). Jesus knows that the time is coming soon when he will be put to death. This was to be a dramatic demonstration of who he really is: God become man.

13. What things did Martha believe about Jesus?
    verse 21 _____
    verse 22 _____
    verse 27 _____

14. What even greater truth did Jesus want her to know about him (verse 25)?

    _____

15. Look at verses 25 and 26. What answer would you give if Jesus asked you that question?

    _____

DAY FIVE:
Jesus – the way, the truth, the life
John 14: 6–14

16. Jesus tells his disciples about his relationship with God

the Father. Read each verse and finish its sentence.
Verse 6b: Jesus said, '. . . no-one goes to the Father

_____

Verse 7: Jesus said, ' _____
you will know the Father.'
Verse 9b: Jesus said, ' _____
has seen the Father.'
Verse 11: Jesus said, ' _____
and the Father is in me.'

17. Jesus does some straight-talking. What does verse 6 say to those who think they can make their own way to heaven and life after death?

_____

 DAY SIX:
Jesus – the true vine
John 15: 5–10; Galatians 5: 22–23

18. What picture does Jesus use for himself (verse 5)?

_____

19. What picture does Jesus use for those who belong to him (verse 5a)?

_____

20. What is the fruit Jesus wants us to bear (Galatians 5: 22–23)? *Remember:* we should bear all the fruit all of the time, not just some of the fruit some of the time.

_____

21.   What future is there for those who do not join their lives to Jesus (John 15, verse 6)?

22.   What does Jesus tell us about his love for us (verse 9)?

 ## SUMMARY

It must become clear to any who seriously look at the Gospels that we cannot hold Jesus at arm's length. Like those who met Jesus, we are forced to take sides. We must either accept him as he is — God among us, the only way to God, the whole truth about God, the only source of life in God — or we must turn our back on him. Certainly, if we turn our back on him, we get to keep on being our own boss, but from this point onwards we will know that we do so against all sense and reason. In the end we will be condemned for it.

To those who accept him as Lord, Jesus is food, hope of a certain future, the keeper and guide of his people. He does not just point the way to life. He *is* life. Without him there is no life.

Jesus' words to Martha are also for us. In John 11: 25–26, he said: 'I am the resurrection and the life. Whoever believes in me will live, even though he dies; and whoever lives and believes in me will never die. Do you believe this?'

Putting our trust in Jesus means a change of heart, not just a nod of the head. It's not enough to believe he can change us. We must allow him to *do* it. Don't be just a head-nodder; ask Jesus to change your life from the inside out.

STUDY NINE:
Jesus – the servant of God

We have thought about the teaching of Jesus. Now we begin to look at the events which led up to his arrest.

Why did Jesus have to die? Isn't there enough suffering without God having to add one more death to it all? Surely it had been quite obvious to Jesus that his enemies would get him eventually. Why didn't he take more care to escape? It almost seems as if he walked right into their hands.

In a way, that's exactly what he did. We see now that the time had come when Jesus would no longer keep out of the way of the leaders in Jerusalem. He leaves Galilee behind and heads for the city. They think he has come with the purpose of taking power. He knows he has come to die.

Jesus is the Son of God, but he is also his willing *servant*. God, his Father, has sent Jesus on the great rescue mission for all mankind. It is a mission which includes his own death. Without that death, the mission would fail.

 DAY ONE:
The servant is king
Matthew 21: 1–11

1. What kind of king had the prophet spoken about (verse 5b)?

_____

_____

2. What three things did the people in the crowd say about Jesus?
    verse 9   (a) _____
              (b) _____
    verse 11 (c) _____

3. What kind of impact did Jesus' procession make on the city of Jerusalem (verse 10)?

    _____

4. The crowd was caught up in the atmosphere of the moment. But if Jesus is our king, our response to him must be more than just emotional. What is the characteristic of those who serve King Jesus (verse 6)?

    _____

✎ DAY TWO:
The servant is Messiah
Matthew 21: 12–17

Businessmen had set up shop in the outer court of the temple. This was the only place the Gentiles, the people who weren't Jews, could come to worship God. They weren't allowed to enter anywhere else in the temple.

5. Look at Luke 2: 49 and John 2: 16. What does Jesus call the temple on both occasions?

    _____

6. How did Jesus show he believed he had authority over what happened in the temple (verse 12)?

    _____

Note: The temple was the only place where sacrifices were made to God. Only temple money could be used to buy what was needed. The money-changers exchanged this for ordinary money at their own rates. Pigeons were the sacrifice for poor people.

7. What words of Jesus show us that the stall holders weren't being honest (verse 13b)?

_____

8. What was the temple supposed to be (verse 13a)?

_____

9. What two things made the religious leaders angry (verses 14–15)?
   (a) _____
   (b) _____

Note: By calling Jesus 'Son of David', the children were saying he was the Messiah, 'the person God sends to save us'.

10. How does Jesus describe the praise of the children (verse 16b)?

_____

 ## Day Three:
The servant is anointed
Matthew 26: 3–13

11. What did the disciples think of the woman's action (verses 8–9)?

_____

12. What did Jesus think of her action (verse 10b)?

_____

13. What did Jesus mean in verse 11 by saying, 'You won't always have me' (verses 3–4)?

_____

14. What had the woman done for Jesus (verse 12)?

_____

Note: She was the only one to have that privilege. There was no time to anoint Jesus' body before he was buried and, when the women went to the tomb to do so, Jesus was found alive (Mark 16: 1–8).

 ## DAY FOUR:
The servant is betrayed
Luke 22: 3–6; John 12: 4–6

15. Read John 12: 4–6 and Luke 22: 5
    What appeared to be Judas' greatest love?

    _____

16. Who was directing Judas' life (Luke 22: 3)?

    _____

17. Just as those who have Jesus as Lord obey him, so those who have Satan in control obey him. What did Judas do (verse 4)?

    _____

    _____

18. The Bible allows us no middle path. We either choose to belong to the kingdom of God or we are in fact under Satan's control. If we reject Jesus' rule in our lives, we are no better off than Judas.

    Think: Whose kingdom am I living in: the kingdom of God or the kingdom of Satan?

    _____

    _____

DAY FIVE:
The servant of all people
Luke 22: 7–8 and 14–20

Note: Exodus chapters 11 and 12 gives the account of how the Passover meal began. It is still celebrated each year by Jews.

19. How did Jesus show his disciples that his body would be broken on the cross (verse 19a)?

_____

20. For whom was Jesus going to die (verses 19b and 20b)?

_____

21. Of what was the cup of wine a picture (verse 20)?

_____

A covenant is an agreement, in this case written by God. The old covenant of the law pointed the way to the coming of Jesus. But now Jesus, the perfect sacrifice, was about to die.

From that time on, there was a new agreement put forward by God. If we want to be acceptable to God, we must come to him by putting our trust in Jesus. We must accept Jesus' death as being on our behalf and make it ours, by asking his forgiveness and giving him control of our lives.

 ## DAY SIX:
The servant of God
Matthew 26: 36–46

22. How did Jesus feel about his coming death (verses 37b–38)? _____

23. What did he ask his three closest friends, Peter, James and John to do for him (verse 38b)?

_____

_____

24. How did they let him down (verse 40)?

_____

25. What did Jesus want more than anything else — even more than his own life (verse 39b)?

_____

✎ SUMMARY

Jesus enters Jerusalem, the city of God, as God's servant. The crowds now have the opportunity they have long wanted: to call him their king, welcome him as their Messiah, and cheer the coming of a new and great age like the one in which King David ruled.

They were *right*. Jesus is King. He is the Messiah. The new age was about to begin — very, very soon.

They were also *wrong*. Jesus' kingdom wasn't to be one which belonged to this planet, tied down by place and time. It was to be a kingdom which began in the lives of people who would bow to his rule. It would be founded in heaven and it would last forever.

When Jesus stormed through the temple sending those who cheated and robbed scurrying for cover, he did so as the one who was greater than the temple, greater than the High Priest or the temple police. He did so as the Messiah of God, who would bring the people back to true worship and a right relationship with God.

The new age the crowds were expecting was not to be one of wealth, power and greatness for their country. It was the new age in which God would personally live in the lives of people. There would be no need to go to the temple because God would be present within them. There would be no need for sacrifices because Jesus was to be the once-and-for-all sacrifice.

The gentle woman who wept for Jesus understood that he would die. How she must have longed to do something to stop it from happening! But Jesus wasn't a victim. He had told his disciples: 'No-one takes my life away from me. I give it up of my own free will' (John 10: 18).

The servant of God became the servant of mankind, betrayed by a friend at the time of Passover. Jesus was to be the Passover Lamb. His death would keep us safe, just like the blood on the doorposts had kept the Jews safe in Egypt (Exodus 12: 1–14).

Jesus knew what he was doing, he knew what it would cost and he was determined to see it through.

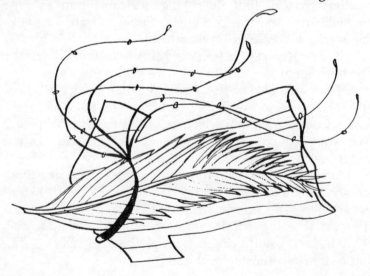

STUDY TEN:
Jesus – the Lamb of God

The picture of the lamb being offered as a substitute for the sin of people was well-known to the Jews. In Egypt, those who painted the blood of a lamb over their doorposts and ate the meat were kept safe from the angel of death as he passed over the land. From that time on the Jews celebrated the Passover Feast. It was the celebration of their freedom from slavery (Exodus 12).

The prophet Isaiah (Isaiah chapter 53) spoke about the coming of the Messiah over 700 years before Jesus. He called him a lamb being led to the slaughter.

When John the Baptiser saw Jesus, he said, 'Look, the Lamb of God who takes away the sin of the world!' (John 1: 29 and 36).

From the beginning of time, God had warned us about how serious sin is. Sin, or self-rule in our lives, cuts us off from God. The Bible calls this 'death'. We cannot make our own way back to God, just as a dead person can't bring himself back to life.

God is *holy*. That means he won't put up with sin; near enough isn't good enough.

God is *just*. That means our rebellion has to be punished. He won't pretend it doesn't matter.

God is *love*. That means he reaches out to us and opens the way for us to come to him. He sent his Lamb, Jesus, to stand in our place — to take our punishment for us.

✎ DAY ONE:
The Lamb is taken
for slaughter
Matthew 26: 47–56

1. Who led the armed men to
    Jesus (verse 47a)?

    _____

    _____

2. Who had given him authority to
    do so (verse 47b)?

    _____

    _____

3. How did Judas use his 'friendship' with Jesus to
    betray him (verses 48–49)?

    _____

    _____

4. How do we know the men were expecting a fight
    (verses 47 and 50)?

    _____

Note: John 18: 10 tells us it was Peter who cut off the
servant's ear. Luke 22: 51 tells us Jesus touched his ear and
healed it.

5. Read verses 52–54. The disciples are outnumbered.
    Their enemies are armed. But who is really in
    control of what is happening? _____

6. Why did Jesus allow himself to be arrested (verse 54)?

    _____

    _____

DAY TWO:
The Lamb is prepared for slaughter
Mark 14: 53–65

7. Where did the armed men take Jesus (verse 53)?

   _____

8. How do we know the Council didn't plan a fair trial (verse 55)? _____

   _____

9. How did Jesus respond to the lies told about him (verses 60–61a)? _____

   _____

10. Read verses 61b–62. If a man claims, as Jesus did, to be 'the Messiah, the Son of the blessed God', he should be able to back up his claim. What are some of the things Jesus had done that proved he was telling the truth? (Look over previous studies, especially STUDY FOUR.)

    _____

    _____

11. If we have made up our minds to not believe, no amount of evidence will convince us. Our minds are closed.

What was the Council's decision (verse 64b)?

_____

_____

✎ DAY THREE:
The Lamb is denied
Matthew 26: 31–46, 58 and 69–75

12. What had Jesus told the disciples they would all do to him (verse 31)? _____

_____

13. What had Peter thought he was prepared to do for Jesus (verse 35)? _____

_____

14. Why had Peter gone to the High Priest's house (verse 58)? _____

_____

15. Read verse 33. In whom do you think Peter was trusting: himself or God? _____

_____

16. Read verses 40–41. What was Peter doing when he should have been praying? _____

_____

17. Now Peter faced a crisis and he wasn't prepared for it. How did he let Jesus down this time (verses 70, 72 and 74)? _____

_____

18. How is Peter's behaviour a warning to us?

_____

_____

_____

DAY FOUR:
The Lamb is innocent
Matthew 27: 1–2 and 11–26

Note: Only the Roman Governor could order a man to be put to death. The Council first had to convince him that Jesus deserved to die.

19. Isaiah 53: 7 says: 'Like a lamb about to be slaughtered, like a sheep about to be sheared, he never said a word'. How does Jesus show that he is the lamb Isaiah was talking about (verses 11–14)?

_____

20. Why had the Jewish leaders handed Jesus over to Pilate (verse 18)?

_____

21. What did Pilate's wife tell him to do about Jesus (verse 19)?

Why? _____

_____

22. Mark 15: 7 tells us Barabbas was guilty of rioting and murder. Pilate believed Jesus was innocent. Why didn't he set him free (verse 24)?

_____

23. In spite of Pilate's words in verse 24 that 'it wasn't his fault', he alone had the right to condemn a man or set him free. What do you think of Pilate's

decision?_____

_____

✎ **DAY FIVE:**
The Lamb suffers
Luke 23: 26–43

24. There were many people at the scene of the cross. Write next to each one why they were there:

The people: **Why they were there:**

Verse 26: Simon from Cyrene _____

_____

Verse 27: The women   _____

_____

Verse 32: The two criminals _____

_____

Verse 35a: The people   _____

_____

Verse 35b: The Jewish leaders _____

_____

Verses 26, 33–34: The soldiers _____

_____

25. Only one man really seemed to understand what was happening. Who was it (verses 39–42)?

_____

26. What was Jesus' promise to him (verse 43)?

_____

_____

✎ DAY SIX:
The Lamb is sacrificed
Matthew 27: 45–61

Isaiah 53: 6 says, 'All of us were like sheep that were lost, each of us going his own way. But the Lord made the punishment fall on him, the punishment all of us deserved'.

27. At that time, when Jesus took on himself all the guilt and blame for our sin, two things happened. What were they?
    (a) *Verse 45:* At noon _____

    _____

    (b) *Verse 46b:* God the Father_____
        his Son.

28. The curtain in the temple separated the most holy place, God's place, from the holy place where the priests offered prayer on behalf of the people. It was a picture of

how sin keeps us apart from God. What happened
to the curtain when Jesus died (verse 51)? _____

_____

29. What happened to prove that death had been overcome (verses 52 and 53)?

_____

_____

30. What did the army officer and soldiers think about
Jesus now (verse 54)? _____

_____

✎ SUMMARY

The sacrifice lamb for the Passover meal had to be a perfect
lamb. It is because Jesus, the perfect man, stood in our
place, that God can 'pass over' our sin and forgive us. He
doesn't pretend we are good. He paid for us with his life.

It was while Jesus hung on the cross that he knew
what it meant to be cut off from his Father. God turned his
back on his Son (Matthew 27: 46). Jesus didn't deserve to
die, but you and I do. Jesus died so that we don't have to
die. Jesus was separated from God so that we can come
back to him. Jesus was found 'guilty' so that we can be
called 'innocent'.

As Jesus hung on the cross, all the love of God, the
justice of God, the holiness of God and the mercy of God
met and were satisfied. John tells us that Jesus' final cry
was 'It is finished!' (John 19: 39).

It was a cry of victory. Sin had been punished. The
way to God was open. The rescue mission to helpless
mankind was a 'mission accomplished'.

But the death of Jesus, the Lamb of God, is not an
automatic insurance cover against eternal death — that
separation from God we call 'hell'. Just as those who are

drowning can struggle against the one who has come to their rescue and even refuse to be saved, so can we. The Rescuer has come for us. If we want to be saved, we must put ourselves entirely in his hands.

It's no use saying, 'I'll let you rescue me as long as you do it my way'. The way of rescue is complete surrender. We are in no position to bargain. We are dead. Only Jesus can give us life.

Ask his forgiveness. Put him in charge of your life. Begin living eternal life right now.

STUDY ELEVEN:
Jesus – the victory of God

Jesus was dead. It wasn't what you might call your average kind of execution. For the religious leaders, it had been a close call. They'd worked long and hard to bring it off, then that weak-kneed Pilate had made a half-hearted attempt to let Jesus go.

Then, of course, there were the strange happenings while he was dying: darkness covering the land for three hours (Luke 23: 44); the great heavy curtain in the temple ripped like a piece of rotten calico from top to bottom. The Roman soldiers believed, but then they always were a superstitious lot.

Now with Jesus dead and buried, they could forget about him and get back to normal. Everyone would soon forget this Jesus of Nazareth ever existed.

But just in case his followers tried to pull a body-snatch job and then make out Jesus was alive, there were a few precautions to take. . .

 ## DAY ONE:
Victory over opposition
Matthew 27: 57–66

Jesus was dead and, while his friends mourned, the religious leaders were making sure he stayed dead.

1. Isaiah 53: 9 tells us the Messiah would be 'buried with the rich'. How do verses 57–60 fulfil that prophecy?

_____

2. The bodies of criminals belonged to the government

and were buried by them. What shows us that
Joseph was a man of importance (verse 58)?

_____

_____

3. No doubt the religious leaders heard that Jesus'
   body had not been buried in the usual way. What
   were they afraid of (verses 63–64)?

_____

_____

4. They weren't going to let that body out of their
   sight for the next three days. What two steps did
   they take to make sure no-one could break into the
   tomb (verses 65–66)?

_____

_____

The plans of people to work against God are laughable.
Great care was taken to stop anyone breaking into the tomb,
but they could do nothing to stop the break-out!

DAY TWO:
Victory over death
Matthew 28: 1–15

5. While the women were on their way to the tomb (Mark 16: 3–4), something of great importance was taking place there. What was it (verses 2–3)?

_____

_____

6. When they arrived, what good news did the angel give the women (verses 5–6)?

_____

_____

7. What did the soldiers do after they saw the angel (verses 4 and 11)?

_____

_____

8. What did the chief priests do that proved they were more interested in protecting their own reputations than in admitting the truth (verses 12–14)?

_____

_____

9. The soldiers were terrified and ran away (verses 4 and 11). The women were overjoyed and ran to tell the others (verse 8). The chief priests just tried to cover up the whole thing (verse 12).

What have you done with the fact that Jesus is alive?

_____

_____

_____

✎ **DAY THREE:**
Victory over confusion
Luke 24: 13–35

10. What were the men talking about as they walked to Emmaus (verses 13–14)? _____
_____

11. Who joined them (verse 15)?
_____

12. These two men were feeling very confused:
(a) They were *sad*. Why (verse 17–20)?
_____
(b) They were *disappointed*. Why (verse 21)?
_____
(c) They were *puzzled*. Why (verses 22–24)?
_____

13. How did Jesus answer their questioning (verse 27)?
_____

14. How did the two men recognise it was Jesus himself with them (verses 30–31)?
_____
_____

✎ **DAY FOUR:**
Victory over fear
Luke 24: 36–49

15. Why were the disciples afraid (verse 37)?
_____

16. How did Jesus prove to them that he was real (verses 39–43)? _____
_____

17. How did he show them that his death and coming back to life had been God's plan (verses 45–46)?

_____

18. What was their job going to be (verses 47–48)?

_____

19. Who was Jesus going to give them so that they could live as his witnesses (verse 49)?

_____

20. That 'power from above' is the Holy Spirit who lives in every believer. What difference has he made to you as you live for Jesus? _____

_____

✎ **DAY FIVE:**
Victory over doubt
John 20: 24–29

21. What was the only way Thomas would believe Jesus was alive (verse 25)?

_____

_____

22. Jesus gave Thomas the proof he wanted (verse 27a). Why (verse 27b)?

_____

23. What new importance did Jesus now have in Thomas' life (verse 28)?

_____

24. What are Jesus' words to us (verse 29)?

_____

✎ DAY SIX:
Victory over the world
Acts 1: 6–11; 2: 38

25. How do we
know that,
even now, the
disciples were
still thinking
that Jesus
would some-
how make Israel a great nation (verse 6)?

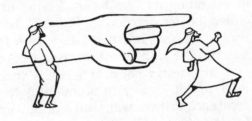

_____

26. Jesus was teaching them that it wasn't important for
the nation to be powerful. His kingdom was made
up of people with God's power in them. Where
was that power to come from (verse 8a)?

_____

27. What would the Holy Spirit's power make them
able to do (verse 8b)?

_____

28. What happened after Jesus finished speaking with
them (verse 9)?

_____

29. What was the promise the angels gave to Jesus'
disciples (verses 10–11)? _____

_____

30. One day, Jesus is coming back as king. He will
judge the world. What, then, must we do while
there is still time (2: 38)? _____

_____

✎ SUMMARY

American author Josh McDowell once wrote: 'After more than 700 hours of studying this subject and thoroughly investigating its foundation, I came to the conclusion that either the resurrection of Jesus Christ is one of the most wicked, vicious, heartless hoaxes ever foisted upon people's minds, or it is the most fantastic fact of history.'

The resurrection of Jesus is the centre of Christian teaching. If Jesus didn't come back to life, then there is no assurance that we will. In 1 Corinthians 15: 17 and 19, Paul wrote: 'And if Christ has not been raised, then your faith is a delusion and you are still lost in your sins. . . If our hope in Christ is good for this life only and no more, then we deserve more pity than anyone else in the world.'

Between eleven and eighteen Roman guards were posted on duty at the tomb, yet by the morning of the third day they had all deserted their posts. It was a crime deserving death, yet no-one was punished.

The seal of the Roman governor had been fixed between the stone and the cave, yet in the morning the seal was broken, the tomb empty.

The leaders of the Jews accused Jesus' disciples of stealing his body. How? Could they have crept up on the Roman soldiers, moved the stone (usually these weighed about two tons) and tiptoed away with the body without being seen?

Or perhaps Jesus hadn't really died. After two nights in a cold tomb, without food or water, suffering from shock (the result of crucifixion), loss of blood from a spear wound in his side and nails through his hands and feet, he revived and moved the stone himself, sneaking past the soldiers to escape.

Perhaps the disciples went to the wrong tomb. . . in

which case the Jewish leaders could easily have produced the correct one.

No. These arguments just don't make sense. The fact was that a band of frightened men and women stood before the very authorities who had put to death their leader and claimed he was alive (Acts 2: 36, 4: 8). They had seen him. They had eaten with him, just like old times. They were prepared to face ridicule, suffering and death in his name.

Christians can know that theirs is not a blind faith. It is faith rooted in fact based on evidence, set in the framework of an event in history. Jesus is alive and, when we put our trust in him, we can be sure that we will live also.

STUDY TWELVE:
Jesus – the promised king

Have you ever stood on a mountain and looked out over the countryside stretching before you? Sometimes you can see clearly; at other times there is a haze or fog covering the area. Some lookout points have a brass plate fixed on a stand with lines pointing in the direction of named landmarks. They are a great help, provided you know what to look for and you can work out which particular object the name refers to.

For many hundreds of years, the Jewish people had been waiting for their Messiah. Sometimes, in the middle of war and exile, it seemed as if they were looking through a fog. How could he come while his people were held prisoners in foreign lands? How could he come when their temple was in ruins and their city destroyed?

As time moved forward, the vision began to clear. Sometimes it was just a glimpse. Sometimes the view was clear and breathtaking. The Messiah *would* come. God would see to it!

We have been studying the accounts of Jesus given to us by Matthew, Mark, Luke and John. Let's now take a step back in time — to King David, who wrote many of the psalms, and to the prophets as God opens up his plan to his people. He gives them his landmarks, pointing the way to his coming king.

DAY ONE:
Where Jesus was born
Genesis 49: 10; Micah 5: 2 and 4

Use the *Contents* page at the front of your Bible to find the books in this study. They are in the Old Testament section.

1. Into which tribe was Jesus to be born (Genesis 49: 10)?

   _____

2. In which town of Judah was Jesus to be born (Micah 5: 2)?

   _____

3. Genesis 49: 10 and Micah 5: 2 both describe Jesus as Israel's _____

4. How would Jesus rule his people (Micah 5: 4)?

   _____

 DAY TWO:
Who Jesus is
Isaiah 9: 6–7

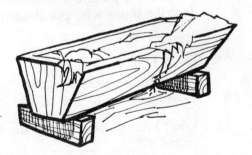

5. Isaiah also states that this child would be the

   _____

   of God's people (verse 6a).

6. What names would God's Son be known by (verse 6b)?

   _____

7. What kind of kingdom or government would it be (verse 7a)?

   _____

8. What would he make the base of his power (verse 7b)?

   _____

✎ DAY THREE:
Why Jesus was to come
Isaiah 61: 1–3

In Luke 4: 16–21, while speaking in the synagogue in Nazareth, Jesus said this prophecy was about himself.

9. List the kinds of people Jesus was coming to help (verses 1–2). _____

   _____

   _____

10. List the things mentioned in verses 1–2 that Jesus does for us. _____

   _____

   _____

11. What is the picture Isaiah uses in verse 3b to describe those who put their trust in God?

   _____

✎ DAY FOUR:
How Jesus was to rule
Zechariah 9: 9–10 and 16–17

12. What kind of king would the Messiah, Jesus, be (verse 9)? _____

   _____

13. How far does his rule extend (verse 10b)? _____

   _____

14. What was Jesus going to do for those who put their trust in him (verse 16a)? _____

15. How does the prophet Zechariah describe God's people (verse 16b)? _____

16. How does he describe God's kingdom (verse 17)?

_____

✎ **DAY FIVE:**
The way Jesus was to die
Psalm 22: 6–8 and 14–18

This psalm of King David vividly describes the events of Jesus' trial and crucifixion, even though that form of execution didn't exist in David's time.

17. What kind of physical pain was Jesus to suffer while he hung on the cross (verses 14–17)?_____

_____

18. Here are some events from Matthew 27. Write next to each one the number of the verse from today's passage in Psalm 22 which foretold these events.
   (a) 'Then they knelt before him and mocked him. . . they spat on him and hit him over the head.' Verse ____
   (b) 'Isn't he the king of Israel?. . . He trusts in God and claims to be God's Son. Well, let's see if God wants to save him now!' Verse ____
   (c) They crucified him and then divided his clothes among them by throwing dice.' Verse ____

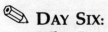

DAY SIX:
Why Jesus died
Isaiah 53: 4–6

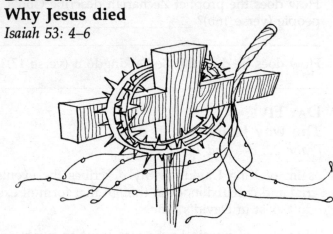

19. Why did Jesus die (verses 5a and 6b)?

_____

_____

_____

20. What picture does Isaiah use to describe us (verse 6a)?

_____

_____

21. What were the consequences of our sin for Jesus (verse 4a)? _____

_____

_____

22. What are the results for us of Jesus' death (verse 5b)?

_____

_____

_____

✎ SUMMARY

Throughout the two thousand years of the history of the Jewish people before Jesus came, God was constantly reminding them that he cared, that he was in control. They were to be his people, his witnesses to the world, the nation through whom he would send the One he promised. The only response he wanted from them was faithfulness.

It was no success story. The nation constantly rebelled against his rule, and found itself under the control of foreign kings and governments. But God was faithful to his promises. When the time was right, Jesus came.

He was born, as God had said, into the tribe of Judah in the town of Bethlehem. He would rule his people as the Prince of Peace. He would be God among us and his kingdom would last forever.

He was — and is — 'good news' for the poor, 'healing' for the broken-hearted, 'freedom' for those imprisoned by guilt, hopelessness and fear.

He is king, but he came to suffer and die. Long before the Roman torture of crucifixion had been invented, King David saw the kind of suffering the Messiah would bear. Jesus did not come 'into existence', as we do, at birth. He always *was* and always *will be*. He is God the Son. His coming had been in the mind of the Father from the earliest point in human history. His was the greatest rescue mission of all time.

But he will come again to wrap up history. For history is 'his story' and we find our place in it only when we find our place in him. We have one life, one time of decision. *To choose Jesus is to choose life!*